WHEN THE MAN YOU LOVE IS AN ALCOHOLIC

Jean and Thomas Klewin

S0-DGG-699

ABBEY PRESS
St. Meinrad, Indiana 47577

ACKNOWLEDGEMENT

We wish to acknowledge the invaluable assistance, advice, and time extended to us by Dr. Leo H. Killorn and his staff at the Alcohol and Drug Problems Institute of Charlottetown, Prince Edward Island, Canada. They not only offered us unlimited access to their materials and library, but also provided us with ideas, insights, and approaches for assisting those who love an alcoholic and must cope with him and his problem.

PHOTO CREDITS: Nick Hutsell, Cover; Camerique, page 4; Wallo-witch, pages 22, 27, 42, and 70; Randy Dieter, page 48; Phil Kaczorow-ski, page 56; Greg Roberts, page 80.

Library of Congress Catalog Card Number:
79-51276
ISBN: 0-87029-149-1

©1979 St. Meinrad Archabbey
St. Meinrad, Indiana 47577

CONTENTS

Foreword

The man you love is an alcoholic! You find yourself linked with him in a unique way, with alcohol becoming, for both of you, the primary focus in your relationship. For him, alcohol is the center around which he has organized his life. It's so important to him he's willing to risk rejection by others, even you, to continue drinking. For you, alcohol is the source of tensions, anxiety for his well-being, and a myriad of other problems. It brings you face-to-face with humiliation, shame, embarrassment, and a need to shift the emphasis in your life and relationship with him, a relationship so strained only the bond of love keeps it from shattering or turning into hate.

In trying to cope with his alcoholism, you may find your goals, aspirations, way of life, and even your day-to-day existence changed, muted, diminished, or overwhelmed by the continuing distractions caused by his drinking. So alcohol becomes the reigning tyrant in both your lives, controlling your relationship and the responses you make to each other.

Yet as an individual and a human being you have the right to live a life with objectives and goals which are truly your own, and to have the opportunity to continue to grow each day as you mature into an ever more complete person.

Because you love an alcoholic and are involved in a strained and troubled relationship with him, it's essential that you refocus your energies and assume the purposes God gives to each of his creatures — to be yourself, to become yourself in a more complete sense, to develop your inner person to your fullest potential, and to set meaningful goals for your life. As you do this, you'll find greater serenity and peace in your day-to-day living.

Undoubtedly you have asked yourself more times than you care to remember how you can accomplish this when so much of you is wrapped up in the tangled, troubled life of an alcoholic. That's why the emphasis in this book is on *you*, the person who loves an alcoholic, and on what you can do for yourself in this relationship to make your life more meaningful, complete, and full, and less frustrating, hopeless, and exhausting. It means concentrating on changing yourself, not him; making your own life better and more fulfilling; looking forward to discovering peace and serenity; and finding ways to grow as a more loving person.

There are two reasons why the focus of this book will be on you and your need to change and grow.

It is the only workable way to deal with things as they are and what you can do about them. This makes it a problem-solving situation for you, one which mandates that you accept as a fact of life the alcoholism of the man you love, and let life go on around his drinking. You cannot permit your love for him to affect your life in such a way that you lose sight of what is necessary for your development as a person — to go beyond your problems and continue to grow.

Then too, it is the only positive and productive approach to the alcoholic you love. It's vital that one person in the relationship be whole and well, emotionally, psychologically, and socially. It is a natural law in all close relationships that when one person makes a change, the other must accomodate to that change with changes of his or her own. Consequently, every positive change you make contains the potential for a positive response from the alcoholic you love. By keeping a positive and growth-inducing approach to life, you are holding open the door for him to join you in living life more fully, completely, and positively.

If you wish the alcoholic you love to recover, you have only one real choice — to change yourself and your approach to him, to cease merely responding to his actions, and to develop attitudes and initiate actions which hold promise for you and for him.

CHAPTER 1
Understanding Your Obligations

It is normal to feel a deep sense of obligation toward the man you love who also happens to be an alcoholic. Perhaps you have had it ingrained into your consciousness and even your subconscious that you have a moral obligation to care for those you love as well as for those in need of special attention, help, and support.

Your alcoholic man falls into both categories—not only do you love him, but he's also someone in need of special care, concern, and assistance. You may feel a kind of special responsibility for him just as you would if he had a chronic progressive disease or a disabling handicap. And if the alcoholic is your husband, you may keep remembering the marriage vows you took to love him "for better, for worse, in sickness and in health, till death do us part."

How then do you cope with the moral aspects of

loving an alcoholic? How much and what kinds of care are you morally obligated to offer him? To what extent must you invest your time, efforts, and yourself in his life? How much trouble, pain, heartache, grief, and shame are you asked to assume because you love him and have a sense of moral commitment to him?

Where do you draw the line between what you owe him and what you owe yourself and other family members? Will that sense of moral obligation which you feel eventually make you love him less, or even turn your relationship into a "love-hate" kind?

Your moral obligations to a man who drinks too much, can be found in the simple words of Jesus: "Love others as much as you love yourself." Yours then, is a dual responsibility—to love him positively and to love yourself just as affirmatively. You can't love anyone, including an alcoholic, as you should until you've learned to love yourself, not in a self-centered, narcissistic fashion, but rather in a positive, wholesome, growth-inducing way. You'll discover your love capacity, including that for an alcoholic, will grow as you understand more fully what it means to love yourself and what your moral obligations are to yourself. Your basic obligation is to hold on to your human dignity and to build a decent life for yourself.

You can begin to understand the nature, scope, and extent of your obligations to the alcoholic you love by remembering what they are not.

You have no moral obligation to play "God" in his life. In fact, you can't play "God" in his life for you have no control over his drinking. No matter how determined, clever, strong, or ingenious you are, you cannot overcome the alcoholic's need for a drink nor provide him with the ability to stop drink-

9

ing. You can't change him, and if you attempt to do so you may change yourself in a negative way as you face the frustrations of being unable to influence the life of the man you love.

Your love, sense of responsibility for someone in trouble, and even your marriage vows if your husband is alcoholic do not mandate that you love, care for, aid, and be so deeply involved in his struggle with alcoholism that you exclude everyone and everything else, including yourself, from your circle of love and care. Nor does it mean caring for him until you have destroyed who and what you are as a person, and isolated yourself from contact with others because you've become trapped in the tangled web of the life of an alcoholic. If he is your husband, it might be well to remember your marriage vows did not ask you to love him "in sickness and in health, even if it destroys me first."

You have the right to refuse to so accommodate to the actions and demands of an alcoholic that you judge your personal success or failure in terms of this accomodation. You have the responsibility to not let him play "God" with your life. Every woman has the moral obligation to dissent whenever the alcoholic she loves attempts to limit her potential by dictating what her life will be and how it will be lived in relationship to his alcohol-dominated life. The woman who loves an alcoholic has a genuine need to free herself so she can live her life to the fullest possible extent. To ultimately help him, she needs to become a more fulfilled, serene individual, capable of growing into an ever more whole person.

Love for an alcoholic does not demand that all your time and energy be absorbed in caring and providing for him. As in the care of the chronically ill, it's vital that you find time to emerge from your caring role for the sake of your own emotional, psychological, and even physical health. Your own survival as a woman, as a human being, demands that you consider your own needs as well as those of the alcoholic in managing your time and inner resources. Unless you draw away from him and his problem on a regular and continuing basis, you may discover you are becoming more depressed, angrily resentful, and socially isolated, especially if his addiction becomes progressively worse. It is comparatively easy to increase the amount of time you devote to the alcoholic as his drinking increases so that eventually your entire life is spent responding to his actions or attempting to cope with his behavior to the neglect of your own life and needs.

What are your moral obligations toward the man you love who has become an alcoholic?

The most basic is to accept the fact that he is an alcoholic, that he has no control over his drinking, and that you cannot keep him from drinking, not by preaching, scolding, waging violent scenes, threatening, punishing, or hiding his liquor in the hope that he will not find it. This may be a difficult step for you to take, because you somehow may feel that part of the blame for his alcoholism may be yours — that you may have failed him or been unable to answer his needs.

Your moral obligation is not just to love, but to love "tough" — to perhaps even go against what you may believe is your role as a woman in love with an alcoholic — to protect, shelter, nurture, comfort, and patiently wait for him to stop drinking. "Tough love" doesn't protect the alcoholic from himself and others by covering up, making excuses, or trying to shield him from the reality of his alcoholism. It means allowing him to assume the responsibility for his drinking, for what he does when he drinks, and the consequences of both. Rescuing the alcoholic may only be intercepting the message he needs to hear: "Your drinking is out of control, your life is in chaos, and you won't find any solution other than abstaining from alcohol." The best way to help him face the reality of his drinking problem is to let him be totally responsible for his own life.

"Tough love" also relates to the moral obligations you have toward yourself. It means you can be honest and no longer need to blame the alcoholic for whatever goes wrong in your relationship or in your life. Let go of what the alcoholic is doing, because what affects your life is not what the alcoholic does, but rather how you react and respond to him. Your alcoholic is going to drink no matter what you do or say. Your refusal to let his drinking interfere with your commitment to live a normal life is not going to drive him to drink. He already has found enough reasons in his own thinking to justify his next drink. Rather than being constantly concerned with why the alcoholic feels the need to drink, you can begin to focus on yourself and to rebuild a normal life. There are most probably other family members in need of a stable family life and healthy emotional relationships. Being responsible primarily to and for yourself rather than responding to the alcoholic allows you to meet these other healthy needs.

If you hope to gain a true perspective on the moral obligations you have to the alcoholic, yourself, and others, it is essential that you learn all you can about alcoholism. It will help you understand the compulsion which drives the man you love to drink. You will realize he is suffering from an illness for which he needs help. Once you have recognized that there is little the alcoholic can do on his own or even with your loving intervention, you will find the freedom to seek help for yourself. To live a life with a measure of peace and serenity, with the potential for continuing growth as a human being, you need to gain the knowledge, insight, and strength necessary to cope with the alcoholic you love in a manner healthy and positive for the both of you.

Only when you have assumed a moral obligation to love yourself in a more positive fashion can you cope with the experience of waiting for someone who doesn't come, of searching and not finding answers, of trying to please and not being able to achieve satisfaction, of loving and perhaps not being loved in return.

CHAPTER 2
Facing Reality

Jane, married to an alcoholic for over ten years, has learned that her survival as a person, able to cope not only with the problem of an alcoholic husband but also with the difficulties emerging from her relationship with him, depends on whether or not she can accept things as they are, not as she would like them to be or as her alcoholic husband believes they are and wants them to be. She says: "I've learned to accept the reality of the situation in which I find myself—loving an alcoholic. I've also learned that I'm powerless to change many things, people, places, and events. All I can change is my own attitude, accept life as it is, and go on from there to construct a better world for myself."

Accepting things as they are doesn't mean you like them, but it does permit you to deal with them and also with yourself.

The first reality you must accept is that your

love for an alcoholic may be persuading you to believe what he tells you—that he isn't an alcoholic, that he can control his drinking, that his drinking is no threat to himself, to you, or anyone else, and that he can stop drinking any time he sees it as a danger to himself or to his relationship with you. Your heart may want to believe this, but your mind tells you not to. You'll never be able to cope with the problem until your heart and mind give you the same answer.

Every alcoholic harbors some myths and illusions about his drinking and what constitutes an alcoholic; so he subconsciously establishes some rules to govern his drinking, rules which, most likely, will also be his guidelines to determine whether or not he considers himself an alcoholic. The rules are many and varied, and your man has undoubtedly used them to attempt to convince you that he controls his drinking, that alcohol doesn't control him. They are his so-called "never rules"—"never in the morning"—"never during the week"—"never alone"—"never before five"—"never straight"—"never anything but beer."

These rules, however, do not mean he isn't an alcoholic; they merely inform you of the rules he has established to convince himself he doesn't drink too much.

Alcoholics have a wide pattern of drinking habits. Some drink every day, others drink every other day, some may imbibe only during the week or only on the weekends. A few will go on periodic binges and then abstain for weeks. If you are going to accept the reality of your man's alcoholism, you need a definition of an alcoholic. Many people's image of an alcoholic is that of a derelict on Skid Row. Yet no more than 5% of alcoholics are derelicts. Most are married, employed, regular people with

15

responsible positions and demanding careers. Some will also be active, contributing members of society and the community, holding down positions in church, organizations, clubs, and community groups.

So how can you be certain the man you love is an alcoholic? Ask yourself whether his drinking frequently or continuously interferes with his social relationships, with his relationship with you, his role in the family, his job, his finances, his physical health. An alcoholic is anyone whose drinking interferes frequently or continuously with any of his important life functions or interpersonal relationships.

Accepting reality also means understanding the nature of alcoholism. The fact that he is an alcoholic is more than a matter of his being weak in willpower, love for you, or judgment. It cannot be attributed only to bad associates, lack of determination, or absence of motivation to seek an alcohol-free life. It's a complex disease partly physical, partly emotional, partly pyschological, and partly social. The alcoholic is sick. The American Medical Association as far back as 1956 officially described alcoholism as a "disease." Accepting alcoholism as an illness can do two things, one for you and one for the alcoholic.

If the alcoholic knows you believe he is sick and if he too comes to accept this concept, he can have some emotional relief. For he can then accept the fact that it is not just a matter of his inability to use his willpower, love for you, and even prayer to find a cure. This doesn't, of course, give him a license to continue drinking. If he's ill with alcoholism, he has a responsibility to search for a cure just as he would if he had any other chronic illness.

If you believe he is sick, you don't have to wait for the illness to reach a critical stage before seeking help. You wouldn't do that with any other illness. The question is how to best encourage him to ask for help to cure his alcoholism.

Facing reality means that you become aware of the compulsive nature of his drinking. Once he's developed a psychological and physical dependence on alcohol he can't alter the progression of the disease because he cannot modify his drinking pattern and habits no matter how hard he tries. For him, drinking is no longer a matter of choice, but one of necessity. He may deny this in a variety of ways—hiding the bottle, drinking alone, lying to you and others about the amount he drinks, and, most of all, denying his ever-increasing dependence on alcohol. He may be aware of the truth, which he strongly denies, of his drunken periods and his failures. He may recognize his need to silence his guilt and he may be aware of his inability to tolerate loving advice, criticism and offers of help from others, especially from you. His continued heavy drinking is not necessarily an indication that his love for you is diminishing, but rather that his need for alcohol is greater than any other need in his life.

Because he is a compulsive drinker, unable to control when, how often, and how much he drinks, there is little you can do to help him stop drinking. Threats of separation or divorce, warnings of loss of job, friends, credit, and home won't stop him. Nor will preaching, nagging, violent scenes, tears, punishment by physical or emotional distance, hiding his liquor, or withholding money be of any use in helping him stop drinking.

There is another illusion you must discard if you hope to survive with a sense of sanity, serenity, and a semblance of a normal life. You may tell yourself he is a different person when he's sober: kind, thoughtful, compassionate, understanding, loving, considerate. The truth is however, he is one and the same person whether sober or drunk. Refusing to accept this will leave you with the unfounded hope that somehow the goodness in him will prevail, while he continues to deteriorate because his need for alcohol continues to become increasingly insistent and persistent. There are no magic pills, recipes of do's and don'ts, or inspirational ideas which will help. Spiritual resources are important, but are not a cure-all, nor is prayer for a miracle an answer. Prayer is your link with a source of strength outside yourself, but it is not enough. Prayer must be coupled to a change in your own life, one which may lead the alcoholic to seek to change his and so meet you where you are after you have become a new and different person.

The most difficult reality to accept may be the different ways in which you and the alcoholic view the world, for there are two worlds of reality involved — yours and his.

Because your worlds are perceived in such totally different ways, diametrically opposed to each other, you must recognize what are asking the alcoholic to do when you demand that he not only place the cork on the bottle, but leave it there permanently. In a sense you are asking him to completely change his way of thinking, feeling, doing, reacting, coping — his way of living and dealing with life. Alcohol has become *his way of life*. It represents everything for him. In asking him to stop drinking, you are asking him to alter his value system, understanding of life, method of coping, in short, his very way of living.

While different types and kinds of men become addicted to alcohol for varying reasons, once the addiction takes hold of their lives it is as if these very different individuals were reading from the same script and viewing the world in the same movie theater. They all see things in the same way, but in very, very different ways from how you and those involved in their lives see things. The alcoholic accepts as real that which is unreal, or rejects as unreal that which is real. He is convinced his view, vision, concepts, and perception of life and the world in which both of you live is real. All of which can only lead him to deny that how you view him, his drinking, and the relationship between the two of you is true, honest, or authentic.

He sees alcohol as no problem, no threat to himself, his relationships with others including you, or to the world in which he lives and works. You, however, believe alcohol is a danger not only to him but also to your relationship with him, a major problem you must work with and around.

He believes everyone and everything around him has been or is the problem, while you see his alcoholism as the basic problem from which all other problems emerge.

He has discovered that alcohol works, that it has an effect on him whose benefits he greatly exaggerates. Consequently he has established a trust relationship with alcohol, knowing it will never fail him. You might fail him (in his perception of your relationship), so might his boss, family, friends, and society. But alcohol? Never! Yet you know alcohol is the great impediment in the establishment of a mutual trust between the two of you. From experience you know he will break promises, resolutions, and agreements because he has a compulsive need for alcohol.

He knows alcohol is an effective aid in his life, because it works the way he wants it to. While he's becoming a slave to it, he believes he is very much its master for he can use it whenever he wishes to find solace, comfort, gratification, and an answer to all his needs. You know, however, that he's a slave to alcohol, bound to it with chains which limit his responses and relationships, especially with you.

He will place the blame for whatever goes wrong in his life or in his relationship with others everywhere but on his drinking. He will use his intelligence against reason rather than with it, and destroy reality with his rationalizations about his use of alcohol. An alcoholic can neither examine nor accept reality as it relates to his drinking, for it poses too much of a threat to his entire world. Even though you understand the relationship of his drinking to the problems he has, there is no way you can reach him rationally, with intelligent observations or insights, because for him to accept your logical and insightful approach would be to destroy the world in which he lives as an alcoholic. He may be drowning, but he won't even admit he's in the water.

Much of the frustration, anger, resentment, disappointment, disillusionment, hopelessness, and sense of defeat which you feel in trying to cope with his alcoholism is the result of these different views of the world in which the two of you are living and relating to each other. By now you have discovered that in his world there are no "forevers," so it's futile to base your hopes on promises and even attempts by him to give up drinking. You have no defense mechanisms to cope with his view of the world and reality except to acknowledge the fact that there is no similarity between his and yours, to understand where he is coming from, and to go on from there.

His wall of denial is so high that help must come from outside himself if he is to regain a sense of reality and recognize his rationalizations as the source of his problems and troubles. He will have to be made ready by those who love him to receive the message that his world is not as he has been seeing it.

You can work to accomplish this by gaining knowledge about alcohol and the world of the alcoholic, and by seeking help to regain your emotional and mental wholeness. By helping yourself, you are, in reality, also discovering ways to help the alcoholic you love. In changing your life and regaining your emotional health, you can create a crisis in the life of the alcoholic—for your new sense of serenity, peace, and emotional stability can make life uncomfortable for him. Alcoholics who have quit drinking report that the loving detachment of those they love made them seek help. They have confessed being threatened because those with whom they had a close relationship were living a full life and they didn't want to be left out.

The prayer of Al-Anon members perhaps best explains how this can be achieved:

"God grant me the serenity
to accept the things I cannot change (the alcoholic and his drinking),
courage to change what I can (myself and my emotional health),
and wisdom to know the difference."

CHAPTER 3
Probing the Spiritual

In your life with an alcoholic, a vibrant spirituality is invaluable, but not as you may wish it to be—the source of a miracle which will somehow make the man you love abandon alcohol completely and permanently. Faith and moral strength, whether his, yours, or both of yours, will not of and by themselves give the alcoholic the ability to totally overcome his compulsive need for alcohol. Overcoming the disease of alcoholism is more than a matter of moral will, inner strength, and a desire or commitment to stop drinking. Alcoholism is a complex illness involving the body, as well as the mind, psyche, and spirit.

Spiritual resources alone will not conquer the problem, but can provide you with the insight, wisdom, inner strength, and security needed:

To recognize the limitations of prayer as prayer relates to the expectations of miracles;

To be capable of a positive and constructive love, the kind which can forgive the alcoholic and simultaneously insist that he assume responsibilty for his own life and actions;

To respond creatively and productively to his alcoholism with a "tough love" and a "loving detachment" — the two ingredients you will need not only to help you recover your own wholeness, but also to do what must be done to change your relationship with the alcoholic so you no longer merely respond to his actions;

To change yourself first, whether or not he ever changes;

To live out the Biblical definitions of faith as the acceptance of the certainty of things that are not evident.

An inner strength, motivated by love and sustained by faith, will enable you to cope with crisis after crisis openly, honestly, and positively, believing that each crisis handled in this fashion can be a step forward in directing your own life and not merely reacting to the alcoholism of the man you love. It takes faith to believe that your relationship with an alcoholic can be changed without specific guarantees or visible, tangible evidence.

In your life with an alcoholic, it is good to hold the belief that "there, but for the grace of God, I might be." It's well to remember, especially when you're angry, resentful, bitter, full of self-pity, and perhaps even questioning your love for the alcoholic, that it may not have been his choice to carry this burden. Many alcoholics live with misery, despair, guilt, doubts about their own self-worth, remorse, and a sense of utter helplessness and failure — burdens which scar their psyches, leaving them emotional cripples. Your man is trapped by his compulsive need for alcohol but is unable to admit this fact because it would destroy the world of reality he has created to accomodate his overpowering need for alcohol. He may, as many alcoholics discover, not even enjoy the taste of alcohol.

This does not imply that you are to feel pity, wear the martyr's cloak, develop a bleeding-heart approach in your relationship with him, or protect and shield him from the troubles his drinking has produced. It does mean, however, that you can love him even as you would if he had some other progressive disease, appreciate your own sobriety, and cherish the freedom you possess to develop yourself to your fullest possible potential.

In the realm of the spiritual you can find the help to do what Al-Anon urges its members to do: "Let go and let God." You can minimize the irritations, tensions, frustrations, and sense of bitterness by recognizing there is nothing you can do, so why not let God be God in the life of the alcoholic? This will permit you to believe that if you are doing the right things for the right reasons, some good will come — either for you, the alcoholic you love, or the two of you. Exactly what that good may be and when it may come can then be left in the capable hands of God. More than anything else, this will allow you to concentrate not on results (keeping your man sober) but rather on actions designed to make you emotionally and spiritually healthy, mentally alive, and psychologically ready to discover growth-inducing stimulation every day of your life.

Too often families have tended to isolate themselves from participation in normal social activities because someone they love is an alcoholic. So alcoholism has become a "closet" disease, not so much for the alcoholic who may drink and become drunk in public, but for those who love him and feel a sense of shame for his actions. It requires a strong sense of inner spiritual security and peace to be able to live your own life at home, and among friends, relatives, and neighbors as well as to remain socially involved in activities and groups within the community and church. For it means being able to acknowledge openly, frankly, and without apology, that the man you love is an alcoholic and not to convey or feel a sense of shame, guilt, or embarrassment as if you are somehow partly responsible for his alcoholic existence.

This kind of spiritual strength and inner security will enable you to utilize two vital forces for making your life whole again and for touching the life of the alcoholic you love — "tough love" and "loving detachment." Some people may believe you are callous, indifferent, unfeeling, full of revenge, spiteful, and perhaps no longer in love with him, because you refuse to cover for him or to protect him from the consequences of his alcoholism and at the same time decline to let his alcoholism dictate how you are to live and what your responses are to be toward him and his world of reality.

It takes an honest, genuine kind of spiritual toughness and resilience to accomplish these two things. It isn't easy to let the man you love discover you've temporarily left him behind, but with an open invitation to join you in your rebuilt and reconstructured life. It also requires a solid sense of knowing oneself to recognize this as the only option you have because you can't play "God" with his life nor totally disregard the responsibility you have for your own life. More than anything else, it mandates an honesty with yourself to confirm that it's love for the alcoholic which has propelled you on this course,

as well as the need to discover a deeper love for yourself so you will be capable of loving him more fully and completely.

Al-Anon emphasizes the necessity of the spiritual in living with an alcoholic. The following are some of the spiritual concepts Al-Anon stresses and which you can utilize in your own life.

Confess to God that you have no power over how the man you love misuses alcohol; that the only control you possess is over your own life. By changing it, you are pursuing the only possible way to gain peace, serenity, and hope for yourself.

27

Practice a faith which believes God can restore sanity to your life, the kind of sanity which is beyond your reach without his assistance.

Turn your life over to God and let him care for you. He, in turn, will enable you to live without fear, shame, or embarrassment because you love an alcoholic and are involved in his life.

Take a moral inventory of your own life and then ask God to change what you believe requires changing so that you can become a more complete person capable of entering into a "tough love" relationship with the alcoholic.

Use prayer, meditation, and the church to maintain contact with God. Look for the insight, strength, and moral courage to change your approach to life and to invite the alcoholic you love to join you in discovering peace, serenity, purpose, and joy in living life to the fullest.

Live one day at a time, knowing God has forgiven the past, holds the future in his hands, and offers you the strength to cope with life in the present.

It is important to stress two cautions in relation to the spiritual and the alcoholic. Don't let a heightened sense of the spiritual in your life deepen his sense of guilt. He already carries enough guilt inside himself. Don't throw prayer and church attendance at him as if these will enable him to solve his problem with alcohol and return him to you a different man. Even deeply religious people become alcoholics.

The spiritual dimension of your own life can give you the insights, courage and strength to cope with the problems you face because you love an alcoholic. It can enable you to love both yourself and the alcoholic with the love spoken of by St.

Paul—kind, understanding, and patient; which doesn't ask but offers; which seeks to accept human beings for what they are, not for what they ought to be or what you may want them to be.

CHAPTER 4
Coping with Shame and Disappointment

Those who love an alcoholic often find themselves making excuses for and trying to protect the man they love. These excuses and cover-ups are designed to help cope with a wide range of emotions, feelings, fears, and uncertainties emerging from the love relationship.

If you love an alcoholic, undoubtedly you've already experienced:

A sense of shame as if there were something wrong with you for loving an alcoholic or that somehow you were partly responsible for his inability to handle alcohol;

Embarrassment for what he may do when he's drunk or because you find it difficult to explain how you can continue to love someone who causes you so much grief and heartache;

The feeling of being on a tightrope because your love for him and loyalty to him demand that you defend him while at the same time you have to recognize that society won't accept the behavior of an alcoholic or condone alcoholism, leaving you torn between your love for the alcoholic and your need to be a part of society;

The need to protect or rescue him from

situations created by his drinking, to offer excuses for his behavior, to apologize for what he's done to others, or to make his environment less hostile or threatening in the hope this may reduce his dependence on alcohol;

Disappointment because he's repeatedly failed you despite his vehement protestations that he can handle alcohol or that he will no longer drink;

Uncertainty about his addiction to alcohol, because you need to keep alive the hope that he isn't a true alcoholic, especially if he's your husband and your financial security is tied to him.

All these emotions and feelings can lead you to gradually withdraw from the circle of friends you once had and from those activities and organizations in which you once participated. If you were accustomed to going out with him before he became an alcoholic, you may now find it unbearable to have him accompany you because he is no longer accountable for what he says or does when he drinks too much. Then there are the broken dates, broken because he either fails to come home or arrives home drunk, unable to go anywhere with you.

Eliminating social contacts is not an answer for you or for him. It will only magnify and intensify your feelings of shame, guilt, embarrassment, fear, disappointment, frustration, and loneliness. It can lead to resentment that develops into a martyrdom complex, the "look what I'm giving up because I love you" syndrome. This will only add to your own personal problems and increase the tensions which exist between you and your alcoholic man.

More than anything else, isolating yourself socially exaggerates the negative influence his drinking has on you. Depriving yourself of regular social contacts can distort your self-image as well as restrict your opportunities for personal growth. Every person needs interaction with others to have the reassurance that he or she has value and worth as a person, and has the capability to deal with problems, relationships, and situations positively and constructively.

Socializing can help you not only look at life more positively, but also better equip you emotionally and pyschologically to help your alcoholic begin a search for ways and reasons to overcome his alcoholism. If you're married and have children, it's vital one adult in the family be emotionally and psychologically healthy and join the children in establishing broader contacts with society. You won't, however, be capable of doing this until you have rediscovered the inner resources needed to no longer make excuses for the fact your husband and the father of your children is an alcoholic. All the excuses you make, all the explanations you offer, are only attempts at facing the truth that you've withdrawn into your own little world because the man you love drinks too much.

The first step in overcoming the feelings which have driven you into an insular kind of existence is to face up to your emotions, to be honest with yourself about why you are flooded with feelings of shame and embarrassment and why you have the need to make excuses for the alcoholic you love. Once you've come to terms with these negative emotions and obligations, you can begin to deal with them positively and constructively, discovering why you no longer need to withdraw from social contacts because you happen to love a man who drinks too much.

This means you have to understand that your

man is sick, mentally, emotionally, and psychologically. In his sickness he can't resist the compulsion to drink. Neither you nor he is capable of interrupting his pattern of drinking. It can help to ask yourself: Would I be embarrassed, feel ashamed and guilty if he had diabetes, emphysema, epilepsy, or any other chronic disease?

You'll discover a feeling of release once you acknowledge to yourself that basically you are powerless to do anything about his drinking. This kind of admission will help you rejoin society and live your own life, rather than carry a false sense of responsibility for how much he drinks.

Participating in a variety of activities and socializing with others will lead to growth-inducing experiences that will reawaken your self-worth. For if social isolation has increased self-doubt about your own worth and lovableness, your reappearance into the mainstream of living will reaffirm that you are a person of worth with something to offer others, and that you can be accepted and loved as a complete individual. This will happen as you find people accepting you for what you are rather than for how you are related to an alcoholic.

You'll need a healthy self-image and a growing sense of self-esteem to not only live comfortably with yourself but to also be capable of challenging your alcoholic to join you in a search for a better kind of relationship and life.

In coming out of your social isolation, you'll discover that in trying to cope with his alcoholism you were permitting his drinking to dictate how you lived, felt, and responded to those around you, especially to him.

Your attempts to make his environment more comfortable and less threatening in the hope that

33

this might diminish his need for alcohol accomplished only one thing — it increasingly isolated you from others and forced you to lose the battle for control over yourself and your life. When the alcoholic is virtually the only contact you have with people, you will be overly influenced by his every action or your anticipation of his actions, so much so that he will be, in effect, controlling your life. The more you try to eliminate all possible reasons for his drinking, the more reasons he will discover to drink and the more likely you are to become increasingly entangled in his web of alcoholism, even finding yourself questioning your sanity, adequacy, and competency as a person.

The more you withdraw from society, the more you will become a shadow of your alcoholic. If you refuse to allow him to isolate you from others, you are only doing what you must — living the only life you've been given, yours. With your resumption of normal living patterns, your alcoholic will find further excuses for drinking. He may criticize you for socializing without him — but he will go out on his own — offering you a variety of reasons and excuses for his actions. That's when you must remember he is going to find excuses no matter what you do.

But on some level your renewal of social contacts will force him to compare his world and his alcoholic behavior with the more normal behavior of others. By rejoining society, you will tell your alcoholic he's lost control over you. Since you are changing, he will be forced to make accommodations, and perhaps he may begin to do his first serious thinking about seeking help to overcome his illness.

Shame and embarrassment may keep you from seeking help for yourself. Al-Anon was founded for this specific purpose — to enable those in love with an alcoholic to share their problems and experiences with others who have or are facing the same difficulties. It may help you to talk with those who understand what and how you feel. Increasingly, communities are establishing clinics, centers, social agencies, and other resources to help people, especially women married to alcoholics, sort out their feelings and emotions toward the alcoholic as well as come to grips with the many concrete problems they must face.

If you are married to an alcoholic, you may be confronted with financial and/or legal problems, fear for your husband's job, problems in your sex life, or difficulties with your children. These may be threatening your marriage or the stability of the family, and no amount of shame or embarrassment should keep you from seeking qualified, professional assistance. Your survival as a person and that of your children may depend on your ability to speak frankly and openly with someone trained to work with the families of alcoholics.

In the back of this book, you will find a list of places where you can seek this kind of competent assistance, as well as resource material to help you come to grips with the problems you face because you love an alcoholic. But you will use them, especially those which require face-to-face contact, only if you stop rationalizing or making excuses for his alcoholism, overcome your sense of fear, shame, and embarrassment, and tell someone you are in love with an alcoholic.

CHAPTER 5
Determining
Guilt and Responsibility

It is not unusual for those who love an alcoholic to feel they have somehow gone wrong or failed the man they love. They feel some responsibility for the fact that he can't control his drinking or give up the bottle altogether. Beset by a feeling of guilt, it is not unusual to ask, "Have I failed to offer him the environment, assistance, and security he needs so he won't have to rely on alcohol as the solution to all his problems? Where did I go wrong, what did I do or fail to do that he turned into an alcoholic?"

The first steps in coping with the problem of guilt is to understand that the responsibility for his alcoholism lies with the alcoholic himself. You are not responsible for his compulsive need to drink, a need which overshadows every other need in his life, including that of keeping a good, healthy, normal relationship with you. Nor are you one of the primary or principal reasons why he continues to drink. He drinks because he's physically and psychologically unable to stop. He has an addiction to alcohol!

One of the most important goals of an alcoholic is to protect his addiction, to deny that he is driven to drink by an obsession he can neither fight nor control. So he must divert attention to other supposed causes by placing the blame for his alcoholism on you, his family, relatives, job, boss, or an endless assortment of other irritations. When he accuses you of being part of his drinking problem, you don't have to assume that guilt because he says it is so. You aren't the cause but rather the justification he uses to continue drinking.

If you are married to an alcoholic, he may, in postdrinking remorse when he is sober, blame you or the relationship you have as husband and wife. Unable to tolerate his own misery, he must find someone on whom he can pin the responsibility for his unhappiness. Since you are the one to whom he is most closely tied emotionally and psychologically, you are the logical one on whom he can unload his guilt. Blaming you rather than himself will keep him from developing a critical self-awareness, one that would mandate he make a change in his pattern of drinking. If you assume some of the blame you will merely confirm what he needs to believe and fortify his rationale for drinking—he is being pressured by others and has no alternative but to drink.

As his wife you can make endless accommodations to meet the many accusations which, to him, spell out his reason's for drinking. For each accommodation you make, however, he'll discover another reason why your relationship is driving him back to the bottle. To accept the guilt he places on you and make a conscious effort to change his environment and your relationship with him will only put you on a treadmill, for no matter how many changes you make in trying to meet his criticisms, they will never be enough for him to stop drinking.

Many wives of alcoholics are plagued by recollections of their marriage vows. Visions of what a wife should be and do may flash into your mind after an acrimonious confrontation with him when he was drunk — "a wife is sympathetic, understanding, helpful, gifted by God with the special talents of nurturing and caring." And what did you do when he came home drunk? You were unsympathetic, angry, argumentative, accusative, perhaps even hysterical, unwilling and unable to nurture or care for him in his drunken condition, leaving him alone and with the feeling of being rejected by you. That's when guilt can wash over you, guilt which says, "If you had tried to understand and been a little more kind and helpful, he might not have felt that he had to keep drinking."

Assuming guilt for his drinking, or accusing yourself of failure to be helpful in reaching out a hand of love to help him handle his drinking will cripple and limit your own life and growth. Self-incrimination about your supposed inadequacies and defects can lead to self-doubts about your ability to manage your own life. To preserve your sanity, serenity, and self-confidence it is vital that you refuse to accept the guilt he places on you or that you place on yourself. Your refusal to accept guilt for his drinking may force him to begin to deal with his drinking with some degree of honesty — the vital first step in his recovery from alcoholism.

You may also have to face the attempts of others to place some of the responsibility for his drinking on you. It may come in the form of suggestions and advice from members of his family, relatives, or friends. They may see your anger, frustration, and bitterness, listen to your recriminations, accusations, and complaints and assume these are in part, at least, the cause of the alcoholic's problem rather than your response to his drinking.

Implied guilt and criticism are especially difficult to handle. Guilt-implied comments sound something like this: "He never drank that much before he was married," or "He didn't drink that heavily when he was first married." The inferences are obvious — somehow being married to you has turned him into an alcoholic. You can reject this kind of implied guilt when you can accept the fact that your alcoholic is sick and would be unable to control his drinking even if he lived with an angel.

Before you can help yourself or the alcoholic you love, you'll have to work out what your responsibilities are to both yourself and him as well as what his responsibilities are to himself. Only then will you be capable of dealing with the question of guilt, for guilt is the product of a sense of responsibility not lived up to. Delineating what his and your responsibilities are in relation to his drinking is your first priority.

Just what are your responsibilities?

Don't engage in blaming others, a maneuver which only keeps you from developing a critical self-awareness of your own faults and limitations and the need to work on changing yourself. Recognize that your unhappiness, misery, and distress are your problems and are not inexorably linked to his drinking problem. You can find mental and emotional health even if he continues to drink — if your life is not governed by responses to his actions and accusations.

Don't accept the guilt he projects in the hope that doing so will keep him from drinking. When you surround him with a blanket of comfortable unreality, you are merely making it more difficult for him to accept the fact that his behavior is unacceptable, harmful, and destructive to himself and those who love him.

Don't blame him for your failure to come to terms with yourself. Learn what is wrong with your attitudes and how you can change. You will have to accept the responsibility for what you do with your life rather than attribute your incompleteness as a person and your limited life experiences to his drinking. Your actions and reactions to his drinking will make or break you, not what your alcoholic does or doesn't do. You may find yourself developing negative attitudes and becoming mired in cynicism and despair. You may be losing faith in the goodness of life and even in yourself. Out of this may come an apathy in which you no longer believe in the possibility of change, either in your life or his. Before you can make a new and successful approach to the problem of living with an alcoholic, whether he's drinking or not, you will have to wipe out this negative approach to your thinking and actions.

When your alcoholic is sober, speak to him directly and honestly of his drinking. He has a right to know what his drinking is doing to himself and others, and you can inform him without doing so in anger or with reproach. Let him draw his own conclusions. If you load guilt on him, he'll only have an excuse to drink again, justifying his intentions with, "You're picking on me." Giving him nonjudgemental information which forces him to make his own decisions about his actions can be an important step in helping him come to terms with his alcoholism.

Force your alcoholic to face up to his responsibilities, but don't place additional guilt on him by attributing all the family's problems and troubles to his drinking. His drinking may be contributing to the family's problems, but some of them would be present even if he was not drinking. He has enough guilt with which to cope just in handling how and why he drinks and what his drinking leads him to do.

Be honest in communicating with him. Let him know what you expect from him. He must decide if he wants to live up to those expectations. Not to let him know, kindly and with love, is to be dishonest with him. If you want your alcoholic to face reality, you must face it first and not be afraid to share your feelings with him.

Recognize that you may be overworked, especially if you have the care of children in the family and have assumed all the responsibilities for raising them, handling the family finances, and making all the major decisions. Don't apologize or feel guilty for your tiredness, mental exhaustion, and even anger because you have all the responsibilities in the family.

Accepting guilt for his drinking or placing additional guilt on him is nonproductive, especially if it involves rehashing yesterday's ills, problems, and unmet responsibilities. More important is how you approach and live each day, concentrating on your responsibilities to grow as an individual and to participate in life.

CHAPTER 6
Knowing Who and What Must Change

Those working with alcoholics, their spouses, and the families of alcoholics are unanimous in their observation that for those who love an alcoholic, the only hope of having a normal life is to institute changes in their own lives without abandoning the alcoholic they love. Why? Because as these experts note: To keep love alive and viable doesn't mean waiting patiently and with resignation for the alcoholic to change, but rather changing your thinking and actions and consequently strengthening your love relationship with him.

You need to change to rediscover peace of mind, contentment, and the ability to cope positively with life. You may not realize that you have also become sick. His sickness is alcohol; yours may be your responses to his alcoholism. Your survival as a person depends on the recognition and elimination of your self-debilitating reactions to his drinking.

You have to live with yourself. Which means you can't permit his alcoholism or your self-destructive responses to undo your life.

If you're typical of the woman in love with an alcoholic, your initial response to the suggestion that you initiate whatever changes there are to be in the lives of the both of you, without waiting for him to make the first step in his recovery from alcoholism may be something like this: "You're asking me to change? You're telling me that I have to recover? From what? He's the one that's sick, at least I've been told alcoholism is a sickness. He has the problem, not me. The only way we'll solve anything is for him to give up drinking. Why should I change? I've been the one who's holding our relationship together while he keeps on drinking."

It is a fact of life that you can change only yourself. However, what you do for yourself in changing can provide a climate and perhaps even the courage and incentive your alcoholic needs to work on his alcoholism.

By communicating a healthy, whole, and vital approach to life, you are indicating that you have found a meaningful world and he can join you if he so wishes. This will place pressure on him, for he will soon discover he's lost his control over you, that you no longer react to his actions.

The deterioration in your life may have been both subtle and insidious. You probably have not recognized or realized what has been happening to you. Chances are, your friends will not tell you because they will attribute your changes in emotions, attitudes, and personality to the situations in which you find yourself — in love with, and perhaps also married to an alcoholic.

Your suffering can be just as real and damaging

as that of your alcoholic—physically, psychologically, and emotionally. In fact, you may often be the
victim of a double hurt. He acts and you hurt. In
turn, you react by hurting yourself.

If you need proof that you must change, take
an inventory of the symptoms of your sickness—bitterness, fear, resentment, guilt, shame, tension,
depression, anger, anxiety, doubts about your self-
worth, and a martyrdom complex. All are related to
the alcoholic you love, but they are not symptoms of
alcoholism as much as they are the symptoms of a
developing disorder in you. Even your physical
health may be involved. Stress and tension can do
things to you—headaches, insomnia, and other
physical ailments.

You need to change, especially if you are married to an alcoholic or if he is your son and living at
home. You have to get off the roller coaster on
which your emotional life is riding. You're high
when he vows to remain sober and abstains for a
period of time. But you drop just as swiftly and
precipitously when he falls off the wagon. Your relationship with him may be good when he's sober,
because then he's gentle, loving, considerate, and
helpful only to become the opposite when he's drinking. No woman can live with these emotional peaks
and valleys indefinitely without having it affect her.

You can prepare yourself to make the necessary
changes in your life by asking: "What if I center all
my hope for a normal life on his recovery and he
never stops drinking? Can I continue to live with
emotional stress, strain, and pressure? Do I have a
right to some relief from all this? Can this marriage
and family survive and remain intact without one
adult member being healthy and whole?"

The second step is to convince yourself that it's

possible:

To lead a reasonably normal and happy life whether or not your alcoholic recovers from his alcoholism;

To make a life for yourself and your family and simultaneously develop a greater compassionate understanding of his disease;

To come out of yourself and recover your hopes, plans, and dreams;

To find a joy in struggling and achieving growth for yourself without abandoning or leaving behind the alcoholic you love;

To believe that for every positive change you make, your alcoholic must also make some adjustment in his life.

The third step is to recognize a few facts about your love relationship with an alcoholic. This means that you learn to accept things as they are. It doesn't mean that you have to like them, but merely that you accept the fact that the situation will not change until he seeks help. All you can do is change your attitude towards the situation and go on from there.

It's important that you discover how to let go of a problem over which you have no control, and that you do it in a healthy, positive, constructive fashion. This means you will have to develop an ability to live and let live. It means you make it a rule for your life that there is no need for you to accept what he imposes on you, even if he is your husband. To spend your time, emotions, and energies correcting his mistakes, protecting him, or coming to his rescue will leave you little time for a life of your own. You can, in love, permit him to accept the responsibility for his life and actions and to suffer the consequences of his mistakes.

Few alcoholics will stop drinking as long as

other people remove the painful consequences of their drinking from them, or permit them to use excuses for their continued drinking. When you react to his actions, you are providing him additional excuses for drinking. If you permit him to blame you or other individuals, situations, and external causes for his drinking, you are only validating his reasons for drinking. If you no longer accept his excuses, he may be compelled to search for other answers, including those relating to himself.

A visible, active life led with a measure of serenity, security, and happiness can have only one effect on your alcoholic—he will know he's lost control of the relationship. He may temporarily respond by drinking more, as if to blame your new life for his alcoholism. But it may encourage him to seek help so he too can have a measure of serenity without resorting to alcohol. If he can no longer participate in your life by making you respond to his alcoholism, he may seek sobriety as a means of once again being an integral part of your life.

It is difficult for you to make this change without help. Help is available once you take the first step of admitting to yourself that you must change and that by changing you can make a difference in how alcoholism affects all those you love.

CHAPTER 7

Realizing
You Can't Walk Alone

Love for an alcoholic can do disastrous things to your personality, emotions, attitudes, and ability to cope with life. Your self-esteem, sense of self-worth, self-confidence, and self-image may be shattered.

Shame and embarrassment, however, may thwart your periodic resolutions to ask for help for yourself and your family. You may feel a sense of disloyalty in making public his drinking problem, because others may not realize he is an alcoholic. You can fortify your resolution by reminding yourself that there are millions of women in the same situation.

Perhaps you are concerned that your alcoholic will respond violently to the suggestion that he seek help. Fear of his reaction can paralyze you into inaction. It may help to ask yourself if his initial violent reaction would be any worse than what you are now enduring.

Your biggest enemy, however, may be your own strength. Your perception that the primary responsibility for resolving your problem lies with you. You can be too strong, brave, unbreaking, patient, resilient, tenacious. Perhaps you've never had to ask for help. Just remember, you are not God so you cannot and do not have all the answers nor the unlimited strength to continue to deal alone with your problem.

If and when you seek help, it is vital that you understand for whom the primary help is intended—you! You may be tempted to ask for assistance to "get him to stop drinking," as if the solution to all your troubles lies in his sobriety. But if you limit your search for help to his apparent need, you may be forced to live with your problems and troubles indefinitely, for there is no guarantee he will stop drinking or even consent to be helped.

Once you understand that the only person you can change is yourself, you are free to ask how you can find peace of mind and contentment, the ability to cope with life as it relates to his illness, and a happiness which isn't dependent upon his recovery from alcoholism.

There is much misunderstanding and many myths about the alcoholic and alcoholism. That's why it is important that you find someone competent and qualified to help you. Begin with an attempt to understand what an alcoholic is and isn't. This will include what it is and is not possible for him to do to stop drinking and what you can do to influence him. Emerging from this will be insights on how you can cope with your feelings, emotions, and life, so that you will not be dependent upon your alcoholic.

The first step in your search for help may be for

you and your family to talk about your "secret," the fact that the man you love is an alcoholic. This will not only permit you to emerge from your isolation, but may also force the alcoholic to admit what he already knows but cannot acknowledge if he is to continue drinking—that he is an alcoholic.

Where do you find the kind of competent, qualified assistance you will need? Al-Anon can help you gain insights into alcoholism and learn how you can begin to make positive changes in your life even while he is drinking. Alcohol institutes and clinics also are valuable sources of information and assistance. You not only need competent, qualified help; you need contact with people qualified in the field of alcoholism, for it's a special kind of sickness requiring a specialist.

What types of assistance do you need?

If you are married, you may require assistance in dealing with the violence alcoholics frequently display when drunk. If you have lived with violence, either verbal or physical, you may have reached the point where you are fearful that any move by you will trigger more violence. Al-Anon members recognize that many wives have been beaten down mentally and physically for so long they are not able to get out of the situation or to find a workable means of protecting themselves from further abuse.

If you've been the victim of abuse, you may have discovered that involving the police is no long-term solution; in fact, it may only make matters worse. Money can be a major obstacle in seeking legal advice and assistance, and a lawyer is seldom capable of dealing with your mixed emotions of fear and love for the man who abuses you when he's drunk, but is kind and gentle when sober. What you need is dialogue with someone who not only un-

derstands the fears with which you live, but can enable you to handle the potential for violence whenever your husband drinks too much.

Since sex is the ultimate and most intimate
form of communication between a husband and
wife, it's essential you look for help if sexual problems have arisen since he's become an alcoholic.
Like other wives of alcoholics, you may find it difficult to distinguish between the alcoholic husband
who is violent, abusive, coercive, and demanding
when drunk and the sober husband who is tender,
kind, considerate, and loving. The problems caused
in your sex life by his drinking may extend to your
interaction with him when he's sober, making your
relationship worse and perhaps offering him yet
another reason to drink. Al-Anon believes it is very
easy for a wife to use sex in such a way that it will
only further alienate her husband and contribute to
the psychological problems which tie him to alcohol.

Few women will be able to talk about their sexual problems in group sessions. But the subject can
be broached so that individual members within a
group, such as Al-Anon, can privately share with
you how they resolved the problem. Private sessions
with a therapist working in the field of alcoholism
can offer you the opportunity to discuss freely and
openly the sexual problems you face in living with an
alcoholic husband. Whichever course you choose,
it's a positive step in dealing with a problem that can
seriously affect your marriage.

If you are the wife of an alcoholic you undoubtedly live with a variety of insecurities, par-
ticularly financial. Most alcoholics bring financial
problems into the lives of their families. Bad checks,
unpaid bills, delinquent loans, and other debts are
an intrinsic part of an alcoholic's life. Since you are

the sober and reliable marriage partner, pressure will be placed on you to redeem the checks, pay off his debts, bring the loans up to date. It may even reach the point where you dread answering the phone or picking up the mail, knowing both will bring demands that you do something about your husband's fiscal irresponsibility.

How do you cope with this kind of pressure and still manage to provide your family with the necessities, when there is so little money at your disposal? Other women have faced the same problems, found the courage to refuse to accept the pressures, and placed the responsibility for the financial problems on the alcoholic. It is a cardinal rule in helping an alcoholic recover from his drinking that he assume the responsibility for and consequences of his actions. As long as you continue to rescue him, he can continue to drink and to act in a financially irresponsible manner.

To find the kind of courage required to force him to face his responsibilities you may need help, especially since your first impulse will be to protect him from the consequences of the monumental money problems he's created. The pressures will continue until your husband and those who cash his checks, loan him money, extend him credit realize you won't assume his personal obligations — because you love him enough to offer him an opportunity to assume his responsibilities, including seeking help for his alcoholism.

Although the alcoholic's condition necessitates that you assume an increasing share of the responsibilities for all the decisions and actions in the family, there is a danger in doing so. While your intentions may be good, they can become destructive when they take from your husband what little self-respect he still retains. In the short run, the family may function more efficiently and reliably, but over a period of time it can only lead to a deteriorating, unhealthy relationship in the marriage. He may become resentful because you have taken from him what little manhood he had managed to keep, and you, in turn, may resent the way in which he has let you assume the burden of making all the decisions and taking on all the responsibilities within the family.

Coupled with your resentment may be a "holier-than-thou" attitude which conveys the idea that the marriage no longer is a relationship between two individuals of equal value and worth, but rather one in which you have become the "better" person, the partner who is contributing the most to the marriage.

Help is essential not only to enable you to structure a more positive life and learn how to cope with his alcoholism in a nondestructive fashion both for yourself and him, but also to prepare you for the future when, hopefully, he'll stop drinking. When that day comes, your problems won't magically disappear, nor will your relationship automatically become a thing of beauty, a perfect interplay between two people who love each other.

You will always be dealing with an alcoholic, drinking or sober, an active or inactive drinker. Even if he never touches another drop of alcohol, he'll still be an alcoholic, a recovered alcoholic who carries the disease within his system. Alcoholism is more than a drinking disease, it's also a thinking disease. While his drinking may stop, his thinking won't. Alcohol is currently his way of handling stress, pressure, inner tensions, and problems. Sober, he'll be faced with those same stresses, pressures, tensions, and problems.

You will need assistance to recognize that his recuperation will be a long, slow process. His alcoholism took a long time to develop, and his convalescence will also be a long, slow process as he learns to handle his problems without alcohol. There will be times when he'll experience a "dry drunk," periods when the stresses and pressures which caused him to turn to alcohol will return and he won't have his traditional method of escaping from them via the bottle. During his "dry drunk" periods you may think things are worse than when he drank. They aren't, because his "dry drunk" periods will pass. Those who have gone through the experience of living with a recovering alcoholic can reassure you that with patience and tolerance these periods can be handled positively.

Al-Anon can be especially helpful during your alcoholic's recovery. Members can explain the physical, emotional, and mental symptoms he may exhibit, to what extent you should let him be subjected to drinking temptations, and how to handle the feelings of jealousy or resentment about the method he chooses for recovery. He may feel a need for almost daily contact with other recovered alcoholics, and you could misinterpret that need — as if others have superseded you in his life.

Because alcoholism is such a baffling, complex disease, those who love an alcoholic need as much help as he does. Your love and deep concern for the interpersonal relationship between the two of you is your motivation in seeking help for yourself.

CHAPTER 8
Accepting and Loving Yourself

You won't be capable of helping the alcoholic you love become once again a healthy and whole person unless and until you yourself have become complete and whole. Even if he should choose not to join you in the search for wholeness and in the process conquer his compulsive need for alcohol, you will still need to rebuild a life of stability, intactness, and integrity.

The first step in once again becoming someone whose emotional, psychological, and mental life is healthy, intact, and sound is to recognize that recovery of wholeness in your life is not dependent on how successful you are in helping him overcome his alcoholism, or how well you protect him from the consequences of his drinking.

Your first priority must be to accept yourself as a person of worth, capable of dealing with life and competent in establishing meaningful relationships with others. This implies that you believe you are someone capable of being loved and accepted. Once you have reestablished this self-assurance of your own worth, usefulness, importance, and competence you will have begun to reclaim your self-esteem and you can begin to establish a better and healthier relationship with your alcoholic.

You can begin your own personal reclamation project by focusing on the spiritual. A recollection of some of the basic truths of your faith and the teachings of the Church will help you recognize what you are — a precious child of God, a unique creation of his, the only one of your kind, loved by God with a special love, of inestimable worth in and of yourself with a special value in your own personhood and life.

You can so easily be too hard on yourself, in assuming guilt which is not yours. You can judge yourself too harshly in expecting perfection of yourself in all your relations with the alcoholic you love, in coping with the problems his drinking has produced, and in deciding how successful you have been in helping him give up alcohol. If you are deeply religious, your conscience may nag you after you've exhibited anger, resentment, or bitterness toward him because of his drinking. If you are married, you may find cause for guilt in how you perceive you have kept your marriage vows to love, honor, and cherish him.

In these moments of reflection, moments which can be very destructive to your self-image, it is important to remember what your church says about all human beings — no one is perfect and no one can live the perfect life. And you are no exception. Because the man you love is an alcoholic, is no reason for you to expect more of yourself in your relationship with him. Loading yourself with feelings of guilt, remorse, and incrimination doesn't help your alcoholic nor will it help you break his drinking habits. Nothing you have done has been responsible for his drinking, and, unless you are an angel with supernatural powers, there is nothing more you can do to stop his drinking. Loading yourself with guilt and feeling responsible for his drinking only adds to the destruction of your self-esteem, making it more difficult for you to live with yourself and preventing you from building a better, more healthful life.

How can you proceed to recreate in yourself a sense of your own worth? The first step is one you have read about repeatedly in this book and needs little amplification here — refuse to accept his guilt. You are not responsible for his alcoholism. He has a compulsion to drink which you did not cause.

The second step is to recognize the limits of the help you can offer him. You can help him only by helping yourself. If you hope to regain a sense of your self-worth by helping him — don't. It won't work. All you can do is contribute to the further destruction of your self-image, for nothing you try can help him. He has to help himself.

The third step is to rid yourself of any self-pity you may harbor. Feeling sorry for yourself implies that you are incapable of doing anything about the situation in which you find yourself. But you can do something, and the sooner you begin to change your own life the faster your self-esteem will return and, like a snowball, the more your self-esteem returns the more you will have found the ablility to change yourself even further.

The fourth step is to stop responding to his demands, threats, pleadings, anger, and promises.

They are all means of manipulation he uses to secure your acquiescence or to have you respond with emotional outbursts, outbursts which, in his perception, justify his drinking. When he becomes the puppeteer and you are the puppet there can only be one result in your life — a weakening of your own sense of self-worth. Review the record of his drinking over the past several years. Examine your responses and recall how he achieved what he wanted from you. Then ask yourself how you feel about those responses and about yourself in relationship to them. Have they increased or decreased your self-esteem? If you are honest you know they haven't helped your self-image, so give up responding as a puppet!

The fifth step is especially important if you are married to an alcoholic. It requires that you do some honest soul-searching, admitting to yourself what you may have been afraid to bring into your consciousness. Ask yourself if there are times when you suspect you're really not worth any more than your alcoholic husband says you are, or implies by how he relates to you. Quiz yourself:

"Am I afraid I'm no longer attractive, desirable, lovable, worth having because he no longer is as interested in me as he once was?"

"Do I feel unloved and rejected, and does that make me wonder if I'm worthy of being loved and accepted by others?"

"Do I still consider myself gifted and smart? Do I think of myself as capable of making decisions, solving problems, being of help to someone else; or do I think of myself as a failure?"

Counselors working with the wives of alcoholics find themselves working with women whose badly damaged self-concepts are the major roadblocks to their recovery of wholeness in their lives. This is especially true if the wife has been physically abused, for the abuse is a visual and physically felt signal to her that she doesn't have much worth. Problems with sex, especially if the husband is unfeeling and coercive in his sexual demands after a night of drinking, can also add to a wife's lack of self-esteem. The counselors note that many of these women have lost so much of their self-esteem that they find it hard to believe that they could make it on their own apart from their alcoholic husbands.

You are not the only woman to feel unloved or rejected because alcohol is the first priority in your husband's life. The message he appears to be sending is clear—alcohol is his first love, the one essential in his life he can't live without. When these feelings wash over you, remember he doesn't have a choice. It's not a "put-down" of you nor is it a message which says that you are unlovable and unwanted. He is merely conveying a truth about alcoholism—that even if he does love you more than alcohol, he cannot choose you over alcohol because his need to drink is so overwhelming it can drown even his love for you.

It is also a pattern in the life of the alcoholic that the more he drinks, the more he loses his self-esteem and self-worth. Since that is too painful for him to admit and since he cannot live with his sense of his own personal inadequacy, he must project that inadequecy onto someone else. As his wife, you are the most logical one on whom he can dump it. The more he comes to hate himself, the more he must seek to have you dislike yourself, because this will, somehow, relieve him of some of his inner pain.

You can work on recovering your self-image by refusing to accept and react to his actions when that would be destructive to you. Your husband cannot hurt you and take from you your sense of what you are worth as a human being unless you permit it. This means you have to recognize what he is doing to you and what your responses will do to your self-image if you permit yourself to become trapped into accepting his rules for playing the game.

The sixth step is to understand that you can regain a positive self-image only when you begin to reconstruct some semblance of a normal life, including socializing with others. The more you move back into the mainstream of life, the more you'll have the opportunity to recognize that others find you interesting, recognize your value and worth, and know that you are capable and competent, likable and lovable. Through the respect, interest, and concern others will have for you; you can recapture the certainty that you can participate in relationships as an equal, with no need to make apologies or feel inadequate. The more frequently and successfully you interact and relate with others, the more you will come to understand and appreciate your own worth as a human being.

The seventh step is to participate and do, for each positive decision and action you take will be a reaffirmation of your own worth and abilities and will also contribute to your growing self-esteem. It may be difficult initially, but the more challenges you accept, the more you rejoin groups, organizations, and activities, the more rapidly your self-esteem will return.

Once you have recovered your self-esteem and self-worth, you will be capable of making a life of your own, one that is not dependent upon the actions of the alcoholic you love. You will have found the confidence to meet the many challenges you'll face, if your alcoholic seeks help and decides to give up alcohol. You will face many crises, difficulties, problems with a sober alcoholic. What you'll need most is the ability to approach all these with a sense of assurance, knowing you have the ability to cope with them.

CHAPTER 9
Finding an Inner Strength

The key to your survival as a complete person in love with an alcoholic is "detachment with love and understanding." Detachment with hate and resentment is useless, and will happen only when detachment occurs because love has disappeared. Love for the alcoholic must accompany your emotional detachment. But, love does not overcome all. Christ made this poignantly clear as he wept over Jerusalem, reflecting that he wanted to shelter the people from impending hurt and harm, but they refused his offer of love.

Your love could diminish, turn into a love-hate relationship, or even die, if you do not find ways to achieve some emotional detachment from your alcoholic. There are limits to how much pain, disappointment and disillusionment you can endure before your survival as a rational, functioning person demands that you cease loving him or leave him because your love for him is destroying you. This won't happen, however, if you can develop an emotional detachment from his words, actions, and responses to your relationship.

Emotional detachment with love will also permit you:

To achieve the measure of inner security, necessary to ascertain what must be done and how life can be lived without producing bitterness, recriminations, resentment, and anger;

To come to a compassionate understanding of your alcoholic's problem and what you can do to indirectly influence his choices;

To render the family a viable, functioning unit, one which can encourage the alcoholic to seek ways to become a participating member of it;

To cope with the anxiety and uncertainty which comes because there is no predictability in a relationship or family where one person is an alcoholic;

To eliminate the quarrels, fights, arguments, and hostility in your relationship so you can communicate your feelings to your alcoholic with love, expressing concern, care, and compassion;

To use a positive approach to his drinking, dealing with reality by exposing him to the consequences of his drinking and behavior.

Through "detachment with love," you accept the alcoholic with love while rejecting his irresponsible behavior and separating yourself from its consequences. This is especially vital since he may not stop drinking. Detachment with love will equip you to continue to love him rather than hate him for destroying family life and hurting the individual lives of each family member.

How do you develop this kind of loving detachment?

Begin by making a conscious decision to put aside those things which are beyond your influence and control — your alcoholic's drinking habits, moods, behavior, thinking, and responses to your attempts to keep alive a viable relationship between the two of you. You didn't cause his drinking and there's nothing you can do directly to help him stop. Keep reminding yourself that your alcoholic is sick, and you are no more responsible for his illness than if he had any other chronic, disabling disease.

Emotional detachment with love is not easy to achieve. It is one thing to know intellectually that you are not responsible for his alcoholism, but it's another thing to have your heart accept this fact. There may be nagging thoughts in the back of your mind which suggest that you are, at least in part, responsible for his drinking, or that tell you there just may be something you haven't tried that might work magic, or that there may be hidden causes for his drinking you have not as yet discovered. Put those thoughts aside; you didn't cause his drinking; you can't make him give it up.

How then do you transmit to your heart what your head already knows? "Let go and let God," is how Al-Anon advises those who join that organization. Take your hands off his life and turn his problem over to God. Once you realize that all the effort and worry you put into your attempts to change the alcoholic will be useless, you can turn him over to God, believing he watches over you and your alcoholic. God never asks the impossible. He only asks that you love your alcoholic, treat him with dignity, respect, and compassion, and then release him to God with love.

Not everyone may understand your "detachment with love." They may initially think that you are callous, self-centered, unfeeling, or even unloving. But as long as you understand that your love with detachment has the alcoholic's best interests at heart, you can gradually begin to explain to others why you have chosen this course. Then too, your newly discovered peace, serenity, security, and ability to function will inform others that you have made the only choice possible, given the situation in which you find yourself—in love with a man who drinks too much.

It can also be your answer to those who counsel, "leave him," if he is your husband, or "give up on him," if he is your son, father, or some other male relative or friend. Separation is no answer for a love relationship in which those involved are being hurt. Detachment with love will allow you to continue the relationship while he drinks and to keep the love aspect of that relationship alive.

Al-Anon, perhaps more than any other organization, can help you work on this aspect of your relationship with your alcoholic. Women in Al-Anon have been faced with the need to emotionally yet lovingly detach themselves from their alcoholic loved ones and can help you learn how to do the same. They can also show you how to apply this emotional detachment to the many particular situations arising from your relationship with an alcoholic in such a way that it will have a positive impact on the man you love.

It may be necessary at times to physically remove yourself from his presence when you find your emotional detachment is being threatened by his words and actions. Take a walk, get in the car and drive to the nearest shopping center where you can spend a few hours just browsing through stores, go to a movie, visit a friend — the time spent away from him will give you the opportunity to recover your emotional equilibrium and restore your sense of compassion and love for him.

You can translate the philosophical concept of love with detachment into physical reality by reactivating your social life. You will know when you have finally achieved real emotional detachment the first time you invite friends into your home even though there is a possibility he may create a scene because he's been drinking.

There are other ways you can be certain that you have achieved detachment with love and understanding. You will know it when you are able:

To calmly discuss or explain to your alcoholic how you feel about his attitudes and actions without engaging in a fight or blaming, criticizing, and punishing him;

To learn to live with his periodic binges without spending the time between bouts worrying about his next episode;

To give up your martyr's role, realizing that it only ties you to him emotionally;

To let him experience the consequences of his actions, without inner fears or feelings of guilt because he has to pick up after his mistakes, thus exposing himself to the shame and embarrassments you have felt while protecting and covering for him;

To allocate your energies and time so your alcoholic won't absorb the greater portion of both to the neglect of your own needs and those of the family;

To offer him an invitation to join you in the new life you are leading, without attempting to pressure him to change his drinking habits, believing that he must be free to choose when and how he will respond to the changes you have accomplished in yourself and, consequently, in your relationship with him.

If you hope to recover a measure of your own independence and stability, and be able to make the necessary personal and family decisions, you will have to learn how to achieve and keep this kind of loving detachment. Ultimately, it's the only meaningful kind of assistance you can hold out to your alcoholic — letting him know that you refuse to be involved, emotionally, psychologically or physically, with him in a world where alcohol dominates every thought and action. He must face your challenge to join you in your world if he hopes to come to terms with his alcoholism. Christ confronted Peter in gentleness and love, compelling Peter to take the responsibility for his actions and words during Christ's trial. And you can use this gentle but firm kind of love on your alcoholic, if you have succeeded in achieving some kind of loving detachment from him.

CHAPTER 10
Helping Children Cope

If you are a woman married to an alcoholic, you already know how difficult it is to create and maintain any sort of normal, stable family life when the man in the family is totally preoccupied with alcohol. Experts agree with you. They recognize that in families where the wife and children must cope with an alcoholic husband and father, deviation from the ideal and normal is the rule rather than the exception. These experts also believe that any family with an alcoholic parent is a sick family, for the responses of the family to his drinking may be unhealthy and lead to emotional turmoil, social isolation, and psychological problems. You, as the sober adult, must not only assume obligations relating to the survival of the family financially and socially, but must also take on the total responsibility for the physical, mental, emotional, and spiritual welfare of the children.

Do not however, blame all the family's troubles on the alcoholic. He is not totally responsible for the family's disruptions, problems, and periodic upheavals. His addiction to alcohol can produce turmoil in the family only when you become totally absorbed in his drinking or permit him to dictate your actions and reactions. The emotional and physical energy you have been literally wasting trying to keep him sober and to cope with the problems his drinking brings into the family could be more constructively used on your children and in the creation of a more stable family life.

Where and how do you begin to help your children live with an alcoholic father and in a family where his alcoholism seems to dictate how the family and each member is to act and react? More importantly, how can you keep your children from undergoing a traumatic experience that may scar them for life?

Perhaps the most important thing to remember is that, like you, they are in love with an alcoholic and struggling to establish some kind of normal life without losing or destroying their love for him. So, whatever assists you in recovering a wholeness and completeness in your life, whatever helps you live each day with a measure of inner peace, serenity, and stability, and whatever enables you to recover or maintain your self-esteem and sense of self-worth can be shared with your children.

Start with an explanation of alcoholism so that your children will be better able to understand what is wrong with their father, what can and cannot be done to help him, and how they can use this knowledge to live with him and still retain a love and compassion for him.

Be honest and candid with them. Don't lie

about the fact that he drinks, or attempt to shield them from ever seeing him drunk, or make excuses for his drinking. It is wishful thinking or self-delusion to assume that the children do not know what has happened to their father and the family. Children have an amazing capacity to deal with the truth. In fact, it's more destructive to them to attempt to hide, minimize, or gloss over their father's alcoholism than it is to level with them about the disease of alcoholism and how it has affected their father and the family. If unhappiness, tensions, problems are troubling you because your husband is drinking, say so to the children. They have a reservoir of compassion. So let them know with an honest statement of your emotions that they are not being unloving, selfish, or unfeeling if they experience the same emotions about the drinking habits of their father.

Most children will hesitate to ventilate their love-hate feelings about their father. You can help them keep their emotional and pyschological health by permitting them to express their feelings and by helping them learn how to live with their ambivalent feelings of love-hate.

You can also provide them with a source of understanding and strength by helping them comprehend that their father is sick, that alcoholism is a disease over which he has little or no control. It will also relieve them of feelings of guilt and self-depreciation to know that their father's words and actions, which appear to be unkind, unreasonable, or even vindictive, are not a true reflection of his feelings for you or them. They should realize that such statements and behavior are most likely to happen either when he is drunk or after a prolonged drinking period when he's in deep remorse or depression.

73

You can reassure them that his words and actions are not a matter of their father being bad, unkind, unfeeling, or unloving, nor are his words and actions an outgrowth of their bad, wrong, or unthinking responses to him. It's especially important for them to grasp that alcoholism has changed their father's personality and his relationships with those he loves.

Young children especially may be inclined to interpret any rejection, disinterest, lack of understanding, excessive fault-finding, or verbal abuse on the part of their father as an indication of some deficiency on their part. You can periodically remind them that his responses to their presence and normal living habits are not really evidence of their wrongdoing. For children may come to believe, "If he doesn't seem to love me, it must be because I'm not worth being loved." Or they may rationalize, "When he shouts at me, it must be because I've done something wrong or have been bad."

From your own experiences you realize what a struggle it is to cling to your self-esteem, to consider yourself lovable and worthy of being loved when so much of what your husband says or does is destructive to your self-image. If it is difficult for you, picture the problems facing your children who are in the process of constructing a positive self-image and must cope with so much that is negative and devastating to their budding self-concept.

You can relieve some of this inner turmoil by reminding them that their father is taking out his hostilities on them as well as on you because he is an alcoholic and not because he hates them or you. It is a fact of life which families of alcoholics must face —alcoholics frequently release their anger and hostility on those they love most. The children should know that their father really hates himself and cannot admit it because this would mean he would have to abandon alcohol—something an alcoholic can't do. So to protect himself from feelings of guilt and to salvage whatever self-esteem he has left, he reacts in an irrational way, taking out his frustrations and anger on them.

You can not only help the children learn what motivates their father to act as he does, but you can also assist them to accept his actions without anger or hostility. There's one factor in your favor in using this approach; children have a natural willingness to tolerate and have compassion for a parent in trouble. If they understand that his compulsion for alcohol overwhelms his love for them, they should be able to live with his alcoholism without assuming the guilt or responsibility for his actions toward them.

If they can observe how you manage to maintain your love for him even when some of his words and actions are unlovable, they will have a model to emulate. Perhaps the kindest thing you can do for them is to teach them how to love their father with a sense of emotional detachment. This, more than anything else, will help them preserve their self-esteem, live a reasonably normal life, find the inner resources to continue to love him, and maintain a viable relationship with their father.

Once your children have discovered how to love their father with some emotional detachment, they will be capable of treating him with courtesy, love, kindness, and respect. They will recognize that he too is a human being, a child of God, no matter what he does while drinking or when he is recovering from an extended drunken period. Don't allow them to be too critical or contemptuous, for their father needs their love and loyalty as much as you do.

What are the guidelines, the "do's" and

"don'ts," for you to follow in creating as much of a stable, normal family life as is possible so that your children can develop the inner resources to successfully cope with life and mature into complete adults?

Do give your children ample amounts of love. They need constant, visible signs and verbal confirmations that they are lovable and loved. Children need shared time with parents, and if their father is too often incapable of doing this, it is essential that you do not neglect to offer them your share of love and affection.

Don't, however, smother them with love to compensate for the alienation you are experiencing in your relationship with your husband. And don't monopolize their time because you have so little together-time with your husband. Children need time with you, but they also require time alone and with their peers. They can become too dependent upon you. This may lead to warring camps within the family with the children aligned with you against their father and your husband.

Don't deny your husband shared time with the children when he's sober. He needs all the love he can receive to fight the demons of self-hate, self-loathing, and guilt he carries inside himself. It is important that the children continue to offer their father love, affection, and support, for, if they completely divorce themselves from him and lose their love and respect for him, it could be traumatic for both them and him if and when he gives up drinking.

Don't isolate yourself, the family, or the children because your husband drinks. Social isolation can make your children overly dependent upon you, limit their social development, and impede their maturation process by limiting their chances to learn how to establish healthy interpersonal relationships with those outside the immediate family circle. You can help by joining them in regular excursions into public life — to shopping malls, school activities, and community-sponsored events.

Do take the time to talk frankly about shame and embarrassment, for children, especially teenagers, will acutley feel these emotions in their relationships with their peers. Let them know that others already recognize their father's problem; inform them his illness is no reflection on them or the family; and reassure them that their friends will be supportive if they are honest and candid about their father's drinking problem.

If you have a teenager at home, he or she can be encouraged to participate in Alateen, an organization specifically designed to help young people find a better, more serene, complete life while living with an alcoholic parent. Alateen can provide your teenager with helpful insights and support in coping with an alcoholic father without hurting his or her own psyche.

Don't enlist your children to help you control his drinking. This means you don't ask them to be models of good behavior, quiet as church mice so as not to upset their father and trigger another drinking bout. This will only produce guilt in them if he begins to drink, or have them become resentful and full of hate because their father is forcing them to live an abnormal life.

Further, don't make a pact with them to find and throw out any liquor bottles he has hidden in the house, garage, and yard. And don't send the children with him to keep him from drinking. This only reverses the parent-child roles, raising doubts in the children's minds about their father's capabilities, while further diminishing his already badly battered self-esteem.

It is a mistake to use the children as confidants, unburdening yourself to them, asking them to assume an adult role when they have not as yet developed enough maturity to cope with adult problems.

It will not work to give the children the impression that you hope their father will stop drinking for their sake, or to use them as a weapon against your husband to force him to give up drinking. To do so will leave the children with feelings of frustration and increase their sense of fear and guilt.

Don't engage in quarrels with your husband, especially when he has been drinking. It can be a shattering experience for a child who must identify with both parents to hear and/or see the two of you engaged in violent scenes or shouting matches as if you hated each other. This cannot do anything but create conflicts within the child, conflicts that are not easily resolved. Children may attempt to resolve these conflicts by choosing sides or, if they are older, fleeing from the house and family to find companionship, peace, acceptance, and love.

Do protect the children from violence and abuse. It is a problem you may have to face—what to do when your husband is completely out of control and threatens you and/or the children with physical harm. You may have to call on an inner source of courage to protect yourself and your children. If it is possible, the children should be removed from the house. Friends, relatives, neighbors will provide shelter once they understand the serious nature of the problem. Physical abuse will not only destroy you, but will also leave deep emotional scars on your children. The taking of legal action in these instances is not a means of blaming or punishing your husband (which is what so many wives think and so hesitate to resort to this method of protecting themselves and their children). Rather, it is a method of protecting your husband from behaving in a way which can only add to his feelings of guilt and despair.

Don't worry about your husband's influence on your children. You cannot control what he says or does, nor can you regulate how he treats the children or the amount of time he spends with them. But you can do something about yourself and your relationship with your children. Many authorities in the field of alcoholism believe it's the nonalcoholic parent who does the most emotional damage to a child, when that parent permits the alcoholic partner to dictate the actions, responses, emotions, approaches to life, and interactions of the other family members. The most positive and constructive action you can take with regard to your children is to make some positive changes in your own life, to find a measure of serenity, peace, purpose, and joy in life apart from the world of your alcoholic husband. Once you have rediscovered these and determined you will not permit your husband's alcoholism to dominate your life or that of the family, the children can be helped to mature into complete, whole adults with their emotional and psychological lives largely intact.

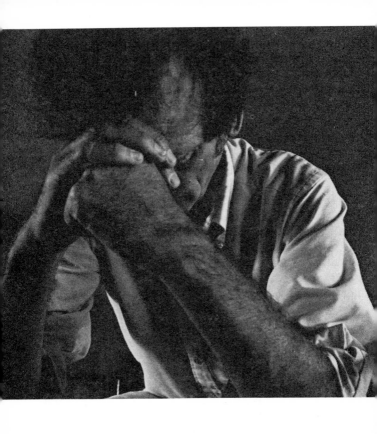

CHAPTER 11
Communicating with the Alcoholic

Because your alcoholic lives in his own unreal world, he can only be helped by messages from the real world. These messages must, somehow, get through to him before he can acknowledge that he needs help and that his alcoholism is the source of, rather than the solution to his problems. Without these messages from those who love him, he has no choice but to continue drinking, for in his unreal world he is convinced that he has discovered the answer to his trouble—alcohol. He has found legitimate reasons for his drinking in everyone and everything but himself. So he will not stop drinking until he himself understands that he has no other choice but to stop.

The messages from the real world must exert pressure on him and expose him to crises from which he must extricate himself, until it is more uncomfortable for him to drink than abstain. Each crisis and every bit of pressure will be a message from the real world telling him, "this is what your drinking has caused." His wall of defenses may be so high and so impenetrable that it will take years for the messages to finally break through and confront him with the stark truth about his drinking.

The messages he needs to hear are not primarily verbal, for he can easily rationalize these away. Nor are they confrontations, shouting matches, threats, recriminations, accusations, or pleadings. These will only confirm his view of reality — you are a part of his problem, one of the reasons why he drinks.

How then do you bring these messages to him, and what are the messages you must deliver if you are to help him?

The first message is a change in your own life. If you refuse to join him in his unreal world, if you no longer react or respond to his actions and instead discover a life of your own which contains a measure of peace, serenity, purpose, growth, and joy, you are telling him in unmistakable language that you have found the real world and welcome him to join you in it. It is a law in all personal relationships that when one person in a relationship changes, the other person must also change to maintain and balance it, otherwise the relationship ceases to exist. If you are married and your entire family changes, there is added pressure on your husband because now a larger circle of those involved in a love relationship with him have changed.

You can invite him to join you in that new life, but you cannot force him to accept the invitation. "You can," as someone has said, "unlock the door of the world to his alcoholism, but you can't force him to open it and come out."

Al-Anon suggests five guidelines for communicating with your alcoholic:

1. Discuss, don't attack. Fighting, attacking him, only aggravates the situation, permitting him to shift the responsibility, blame, and guilt for his drinking from himself to you. When he is sober, he's probably also acutely sensitive to criticism. His feelings of guilt and self-loathing have caused him to brace himself for rejection, and any attack you make on him will merely confirm what he has already rationalized in his mind — you don't love him and are part of his drinking problem.

If you have a grievance, something you want to tell him, let him know about it without becoming emotional or threatening. Do it dispassionately, as a matter of fact, or "I thought you'd want to tell you how I feel about what has happened."

2. Keep your voice low and pleasant. When feelings and emotions run high, voices tend to become high pitched and loud; this would indicate to him you are blaming him for the problems between the two of you. If anything you say triggers a loud-voiced response from him, break off the discussion and leave the room if necessary. This may initially infuriate him, but eventually your responses should convince him that your and his shouting days are over.

3. Stick to the subject. Don't utilize a discussion with him when he's sober to bring up events of the past, items you have saved from the times he was too drunk to hold a conversation or remember what you said. His self-esteem is too battered to permit a wholesale attack on his actions as an alcoholic.

4. Listen to his complaints. Perhaps he is telling you something you need to know to make yourself a more complete person. By remaining open-

minded, reasonable, and responsive you are showing him how to accept criticism with a measure of serenity and security in your rediscovered self-worth. It just might lead him to question his own fragile and bruised self-image.

5. Don't make demands. Make your point without moralizing or outlining for him what he should do to resolve the problem. Give him the freedom to work out a solution on his own. Any positive solution on his part will be one of a long line of successes he will need to rebuild his self-image to where he'll feel confident to tackle the real problem — his drinking. If he doesn't want to do something about it, your demands will not accomplish anything except to further his suspicions that the troubles in his life are being imposed on him by others.

Be honest with him in your communications. Let him know what you expect from him. He will have to decide if he wants to live up to your expectations. It is basically dishonest not to let him know how you feel and what you expect your relationship to be. If you want your alcoholic to face reality, you must first face it and not be afraid to level with him, to share your feelings, to let him know how much you want him to be a part of the new life you have found. Do not, however, make your expectations so demanding, so impossible for him to meet with his battered ego, that he won't attempt to take the first step in meeting you. Your communications must be geared to what he can handle so that the defensive mechanism which permits him to justify his drinking at the slightest provocation (as he may perceive it) will not launch him into another drinking binge.

You can inform him that you are concerned about his drinking, that you love and care for him, but won't join him in the world he has created with his alcoholism. This may imply a risk, but not to risk is to fail to reach out to the man you love.

Your actions can also be a positive form of communication, especially if they say, "I respect your right to live your life as you want to, but that also means you must respect my right to live my life as I believe best. I don't believe allowing my life to center around your drinking is best for me nor will it offer me the chance to grow and live at peace with myself."

If you are married, this means holding to the plans you have announced. If dinner is to be served at 6:00 p.m., put it on the table, whether or not he's home. If you have told him about a shopping trip to the supermarket or mall, don't wait for him to arrive home or be sober before you carry out your intentions.

Whether the alcoholic is your husband, son, family member, relative, or friend, you can communicate your intentions of living in your world rather than his by initiating activities and participating in social functions rather than building your life around his drinking needs. If you are invited to the home of a friend, go alone if he doesn't arrive home on time or comes home drunk. If you have the courage to go without him, you also have the courage to inform your friends why you have come alone.

You can also communicate your invitation that he join you in the real world by allowing him to participate fully in the crises he creates with his drinking. As long as you continue to rescue him, shield him from the painful effects of his drinking, or intercede for him when the crisis involves others, you are permitting him to remain safe and secure in his own world of alcoholism. It is only when the consequences of his drinking are more painful than the causes which drive him to drink that he will look for help. When you force him to experience all the consequences of his drinking, you are compelling him to look at what his drinking is doing to him and to you. Crises attack the defenses he has built to protect his drinking, and it is possible that enough crises endured over a long period of time may eventually breach those defenses. You need to maintain the hope that someday a crisis, whether small or large, will break into his unreal world, causing him to see the truth about his drinking and propelling him to seek help.

If apologies are to be made for his actions at a social gathering or in your home when others are present, let him apologize. If he has broken furniture at home in a fit of rage, let him know, dispassionately and quietly, that he has the responsibility to repair or replace it. Don't call his employer and lie about his need to be absent from work. Do not make good his bad checks, pay his debts, locate his lost car, nurse his hangover, pick him up off the floor, or protect him in any other way. You are only making his life as an alcoholic manageable, tolerable, livable, for you are keeping him from grasping just how bad off he is as an alcoholic. As long as you continue this kind of intervention in his life, he will never feel the need to stop drinking.

In confronting him with reality, report factually and then drop the subject. Let him know what his drinking has led to each time he drinks. Don't, however, make it a cumulative listing of past drunken periods. You can, as you report, express your concern for him and let him know that his actions indicate a need for some kind of outside assistance to put his life back in focus. Do not let him place the blame elsewhere. Let him know that no matter what anyone else said, did, or didn't do, you are talking about his actions when he was drunk. Approaching him in this fashion forces him to make judgments about his drinking. He can reject yours, but cannot very easily reject his own.

You may feel that love compels you to accept the responsibility of caring for him, especially if he is your husband and you recall the words of your marriage vows "to love, honor, and cherish." To love and cherish him may necessitate that you develop a "tough love," the kind which recognizes that it is more compassionate and helpful to let him pick up after his own mistakes than it is to protect him. Love must prompt you to tell him, "You did it, it's your responsibility, not mine." Let him know that you will help him go for treatment, that you'll go with him if he just wants to talk with someone about his drinking. "Tough love" will willingly do anything to help him overcome his compulsive need to drink, but it will not willingly do anything to relieve him of the consequences of his drinking.

If he is your husband, the greatest temptation to intervene will come when his job is threatened by his drinking and the family faces the prospect of no money. If you are tempted to get him out of trouble "just this one time," remember that doing so will not solve his drinking problem nor alter how his drinking affects his ability to hold a job. As his drinking becomes more frequent, more severe, and more prolonged, he will most likely be unable to hold his job anyway. You might talk with his employer; tell him of your husband's problem. He may be able to help get your husband to treatment.

Don't extract or accept promises from him. He

can't keep them and broken promises only heighten his sense of inadequacy or failure. They may even add to his feeling that he is unworthy of being helped. By not accepting and not asking for promises from your alcoholic, you are conveying a very important message to him. You are telling him that he is too sick for promises to hold out any hope for his recovery, that the only solution is to seek treatment.

Since your alcoholic already suffers from feelings of guilt beyond anything you might imagine, accusations, recriminations, and pointed comments about his failures, neglect of family and friends, and social errors are wasted effort. They won't prod him into searching for treatment. The "if you loved me" approach is, perhaps, the most dangerous, for it can cause more damage to his already wounded ego than anything else. Love has nothing to do with his alcoholism. He cannot control his alcoholism by sheer willpower, and even his love for you can't overcome his need to drink.

Let him communicate his feelings when he feels he is heading toward another drinking bout. Help him talk about his need to use alcohol to cope with what he has internalized. If he knows you love him, understand his compulsive need to drink, and will not be judgemental, he will be able, with some encouragement from you, to talk about the pressures building inside him. The more often you invite him to express his feelings about what builds into an irresistable urge to drink, the more you are helping him recognize his need for treatment. This will accomplish far more than trying to talk him out of drinking or attempting to stop him with diversionary tactics.

When he does talk about looking for treatment,

be casually sympathetic. Let him do the talking, the unburdening. He has to bring everything he feels out into the open—his desperation, despair, grief, guilt. When he asks, "What should I do?" propose a variety of treatment possibilities, let him select where he chooses to go for help. Remember he cannot be forced to go even when he expresses a need for help. Whatever decision is reached, whatever course of action is decided upon, and whatever time is selected to make the first step—it is of utmost importance that your alcoholic be acting freely, without any coercion from you or anyone else.

CHAPTER 12
Facing the Future

Your problems will not end when he stops drinking. Alcoholism is a lifelong disease and the man you love will have to constantly work hard at remaining sober. He will need encouragement to continue in therapy, if this is how he solves his problem of alcoholism, to regularly participate in AA, if that organization helps him overcome his need to drink.

Al-Anon reminds its members that, during his recuperation time, the motto you have to live by is: "Easy does it." Do not expect immediate recovery or an instantly trouble-free relationship. Your man will not suddenly be at peace with himself and capable of making every major decision with which he's confronted. His alcoholism took a long time to develop and in the process he lost much of his self-confidence, ability to cope with problems, and the social skills he needs to relate well with others. Someone has compared the recovered alcoholic to a child learning how to walk—he'll stumble, fall, and pick himself up again. Patience is what your love can contribute to his recovery.

Your relationship will have to go through some painful adjustments. You may have assumed all the responsibilities while he was drinking, and now you must and should share them with him. To continue to exclude him from the decision-making responsibilities within the relationship or family is to reaffirm what he battled to overcome in his alcoholism—his lack of confidence, sense of personal failure, absence of worth, and tarnished self-esteem.

It might be well to remember that if your embrace of a new life caused a change in him, then his newly gained sobriety will call for a change in you, if your relationship with him is to be what it once was.

Many wives in Al-Anon have confessed feelings of jealousy and resentment over the method of recovery their husbands have chosen. Many alcoholics, for example, need daily or frequent contact with other recovered alcoholics to keep from taking a drink. These wives have said that at times during the recovery things seemed worse than in his drinking days. But their advice is: "Remember, they aren't really worse. Patience and tolerance, understanding of what he's going through in his recovery process, will help you adjust to the 'new man.' "

The motto of Al-Anon, so helpful when he was drinking, is also invaluable when he is recovering: "Let go and let God." Your man will be discovering a new life, finding new meaning in each day, and he must be allowed to do it his own way. It is what you have prayed for and worked towards, something you wanted so badly you were willing to endure heartache, pain, and all the other accompanying emotions. During the time of his recovery, your anguish and pain will not be gone, but you can be sustained by turning him and his struggle over to a power greater than yours, secure in the conviction that you have done all you can do.

But, what if he never gives up alcohol? You still have a responsibility for a life placed in your hands by God—your own. As a child of God you have an obligation to care for that life, to treat it with compassion and love.

Dealing with your alcoholic and his alcoholism requires that you work day by day on the greatest challenge you will ever face, with no assurance you will ever see positive results from your efforts. You will only be able to measure in retrospect the success of your new approach to your life and his. This means that changing yourself and your relationship with your alcoholic will have to be undertaken on faith and hope. But this can offer the greatest reward and inner satisfaction you will ever know.

Your task is to pursue the creation of a vital life for yourself and for your family, even though the man you love continues to drink. There is a sense of deep personal fulfillment in struggling with life and overcoming without losing your identity, purpose, and goals to the world of the alcoholic.

You will have to remember that this is not a selfish approach to living, nor is it an abandonment of the alcoholic you love. You cannot really love him until you have learned to love yourself, to demand respect, consideration, opportunity, peace, and serenity for yourself. Only then can you begin to realistically expect your alcoholic to find the same.

Your recovery is not tied to his recovery from alcoholism. You can find a better life even while your alcoholic is drinking, you will discover ways to deepen your love for him by having the courage and faith to give up trying to control his life and drinking, by admitting that his alcoholism is a compulsion over which neither of you has control, by setting out to change your own life, and by turning him over to God with love.

WHERE TO LOOK
FOR HELP

ORGANIZATIONS:

Alcoholics Anonymous, Al-Anon, Alateen:
Check the yellow pages of your telephone directory. AA can give you a number to contact for Al-Anon and Alateen if those numbers are not listed. You may find phone numbers for these organizations in the main section of the directory. Newspapers usually carry such listings in the classified ads, under "Personal." If these efforts fail, you can contact national headquarters and ask for the group nearest you:

    * Alcoholics Anonymous World Services
    P.O. Box 459, Grand Central Station
    New York, New York 10017

    *Al-Anon Family Group Headquarters
    (also for Alateen information)
    P.O. Box 182, Madison Square Station
    New York, New York 10010

National Council of Alcoholism:
Check your telephone directory. If you don't find a listing, contact:

National Council on Alcoholism
733 Third Avenue
New York, New York 10017

National Clearing House for Alcohol Information:
A federal government agency that can provide helpful information. Contact:

National Clearinghouse
for Alcohol Information
Box 2345
Rockville, Maryland 20852

FURTHER READINGS:

There are so many books, pamphlets, and journals, dealing with alcoholism. The following list suggests a few resources and titles that might be especially helpful. Many others titles have been omitted which are equally valuable.

Alcoholics Anonymous, Al-Anon, Alateen literature is available at meetings or write to the addresses noted under "Organizations."

Hazelden Books has a number of helpful books and pamphlets available from Box 176, Center City, Minnesota 55012. You can obtain a full catalog, including prices and information about ordering, by sending a card to this address.

Especially Helpful Books:
Al-Anon Family Group. *The Dilemma of the Alcoholic Marriage*. 4'th rev. ed. New York: Al-Anon Family Group Headquarters, 1977.

_____*Living with an Alcoholic*. rev. ed. New York: Al-Anon Family Group Headquarters, 1978.

Maxwell, Ruth. *The Booze Battle*. New York: Praeger Publishers, 1976.

Other books and material can be obtained at your local library or by contacting local social agencies that work with families of alcoholics. The yellow pages of your telephone directory will list a wide variety of organizations under "Social Service Organizations." You might also consult church-related family agencies which can assist you in obtaining material and direct you to sources where you can obtain help.